LEAVE YOURSELF ALONE

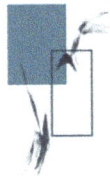

Zen and the Art of Acting

LEAVE YOURSELF ALONE

Zen and the Art of Acting

BY CHRIS FIELDS

Camden High Street Books
11785 Laurelwood Dr.
Studio City, CA 91604

Library of Congress Cataloguing-in-Publication Data is available.

Print ISBN: 978-1-964887-03-6
eBook ISBN: 978-1-964887-04-3

First Paperback Edition, November 2025

Cover Design by Penni Auster

Printed in the United States of America
Los Angeles, CA
www.chrisfieldsactingstudio.com

For Willa and Sofia.

Thanks to Jim Gold, Alexander Bellow, Stella Adler, Robert Lewis, Caymichael Patten, Ronnie Stewart, Chuck Jones, Fred Kareman, Wynn Handmann, Patricia Shingetsu Guzy, Tom Dharma Joy Reichert, Roshi Merle Kodo Boyd, Roshi Kip Ryodo Hawley and Roshi Wendy Egyoku Nakao.

And to all my students.

This wouldn't have happened without Randy Finch, Yusuf Toropov, Erik Patterson, and Penni Auster.

TABLE OF CONTENTS

"It is never apart from you right where you are."

- Dōgen Zenji

"Act before you think."

- Fred Kareman

INTRODUCTION

ONLY LOVE...THERE IS NO ONE IN THE BOAT

*Whatever gains I made were always due to love
and nothing else.*
     -Henderson the Rain King, Saul Bellow

When I was six years old, I happened to put on a recording of Mozart's piano concerto number 19, and I could not stop listening to the first movement. I lifted the needle and put it back down at the beginning, again and again and again.

When I was in second grade, my father took me to see the Bristol Old Vic production of *Hamlet* that had come to New York. I was thrilled by the fog shrouded parapets of Elsinore, terrified by the ghost, intoxicated by all that language. I was enthralled and inspired. Of course, I spent the next few weeks chasing my friend Ben Geraty around the playground at school hollering, "What ho Horatio!" at him.

I wanted it. To be inside it; to do that; to be all the exquisite beauty and order of Mozart. And the poetry and drama of Shakespeare. And I did indeed go about trying, first with music and then eventually with theater.

Ups, downs, and all arounds, I rolled the heavy rock up the steep career slope. I won't attempt to summarize but things were fine; I wasn't a star or wealthy, but I was a working actor and, as they say, I was paying the rent. Except, well, I was miserable. Sometimes I was okay with being miserable and at others, it was excruciating. I had quit drinking and smoking; I went to the shrink. I wasn't a basket case, and I never gave up, but I was sad and angry and could be destructive in ways that I couldn't seem to escape despite all my insights.

In 1994, I was acting in a workshop of *An Undivided Heart*, a play by Yusuf Toropov, at the O'Neill Playwright's Conference up in Waterford, Connecticut. In the play, the town's aquifer had been polluted by a big company and people were dying from cancer. At the same time, there was a priest molesting children in the parish. Toxicity both literal and spiritual. Mike, a young priest, is trying to expose the pederast priest. At one point, desperate and in spiritual anguish, he seeks out a

Zen teacher, Janice, for guidance. When he finds her, she's giving a talk:

JANICE

The monks in a monastery are in the main hall fighting over who owns a cat. The master of the place walks in, seizes the cat, takes out a knife, and says, 'Give me your enlightened speech or I will kill this cat!' No one says anything. Without any hesitation the master slices the cat in two. If we had been there, what could we have said? Big question. Very big. Only great love can answer that. The best way to go at a question like this is not to try to solve, not to look at it from any angle. The best way is to admit that you are completely stuck. When you have no idea, the real work can begin.

He then approaches her:

JANICE

Cat in this hand. Knife in this hand. Three tries to save the life of this cat. What can you say?

MIKE

Please don't kill the cat.

JANICE

Strike one.

MIKE

You're not really holding a cat.

JANICE

True. Also, desperate bullshit. Strike two.

(*Silence.*)

MIKE

(*Makes no response.*)

JANICE

Strike three swinging.

(*She mimes cutting the cat in two*).

Silence does not save this cat. Silence kills this cat. Only love will answer this question. Jesus said, when someone strikes you, turn the other cheek... But this is not martyrdom or holiness or any kind of high-class advice that Jesus gives us. This is seeing our obstacle with great love and with no division.

Mike eventually uncovers the bad priest; but in so doing, is forced to leave the priesthood. At the end, Janice is dying, and he visits her:

MIKE

You gave me the puzzle. I figured it out.

JANICE

Puzzle?

MIKE

Yes. The puzzle. What it takes to save the cat. I figured it out.

JANICE

Prove it. (Pause.) Cat in this hand. Knife in this hand. What do you say?

MIKE

Kill me instead.

(She smiles.)

Then when he tells her that he's left the priesthood:

JANICE

You still pray, right? (He nods.) When you pray, just pray. When I sit [meditate], I'll just sit. That's our bargain. Praying time, only pray. Sitting time, only sit.

MIKE

Yeah. Get better.

JANICE

Sure.

MIKE

Promise me.

JANICE

I promise. (*Pause.*) Right answers. Wrong answers. Okay. I promise. You're so used to worrying about people. But we come for a while. We go for a while. Just listen. You have a bucket with water to carry. At night you can see the moon in it. You walk down the road. Then the bucket breaks and the water falls out. Is the moon, okay? Everything is a kind of mirror, even though nothing looks the same. You and I could shine off each other forever, couldn't we.

Every show, I would watch that scene from the wings and cry. I had no idea how deep a home Nansen and his cat and the moon reflected in the bucket of water—all that Janice said—had found in me.

Then in 2008, I was directing Kate Robin's *What They Have* at South Coast Rep; a very funny, poignant look at how we are unable to love what we have while coveting what we don't; how we cause suffering as we attempt to soothe ourselves.

At one point, Jonas, who is successful and possesses a lot yet is still unhappy, seeks out a Zen teacher:

ALLAN KOZAN KATZ

Many of you have heard the story of the old fisherman who is out at dawn on a foggy day when another boat crashes into his boat, causing the water to leak into his boat. He spends the whole day cursing the careless sailor whose boat hit his then careened off into the fog without a word of apology. He works himself up into a rage that this other man is out on the water causing destruction and pain, threatening his life and livelihood. He spends the day looking for this boat that has attacked his own and finally, at the end of the day, he sees the boat and approaches it, eager to chastise the sailor. But when he gets to the offending boat, he sees that it is empty. No one was at fault. No one has offended or attacked him. Something simply happened. As soon as the fisherman realizes this, he is freed from his rage and his upset. This is like life. When we think someone or something is to blame for our suffering, or that there is even an explanation, a logic to it, we suffer more. When we can accept that there is no one in the other boat, we are free.

(PAUSE. JONAS RAISES HIS HAND.
KOZAN NODS AT HIM.)

JONAS

But what about when there is someone in the
boat?

ALLAN KOZAN KATZ

There is never anyone in the boat.

JONAS

But what about when there is. When someone
is driving on pain medication, and they hit you.
Or when someone in charge lies to a country
and takes the country to war. When someone
goes into a school and guns down all the
children with a rifle. Shouldn't we be angry and
stop these people? When there is a sailor in the
boat?

ALLAN KOZAN KATZ

Even when there is a sailor in the boat, there is
no sailor in the boat.[1]

I identified with the fisherman. I realized that I'd
been putting someone in the other boat and
chasing them, wanting to hit them with an oar for a

---

[1] *What They Have.* P. 64. Kate Robin. Samuel French.

long, long time. So much blame and anger and hurt.

Without thinking, I went online, found the Zen Center of Los Angeles and early one Sunday morning, I went down to their home in Koreatown to take the Zen Practice 1 class. A woman named Luminous-Heart Thompson taught us the basics of Zen meditation. I couldn't pretzel my legs the ways that she suggested, and I was horribly self-conscious, but I felt profoundly that I'd been waiting my whole life to be there and to do that.

It was like seeing Hamlet or hearing the Mozart; like a puzzle piece finding its place. And as I continued to meditate and study Zen, I came to perceive the uncanny and stunning parallels between Zen practice and acting; that painting or music making, writing or dance, any artistic pursuit, is ultimately a spiritual pursuit. This little book is about those discoveries; an offering about the possibility of working and living a life free of suffering.

I managed to drop the oar that had always been in my hands.

1

THE SCRIPT AND THE THREE TENETS

I think 99 times and find nothing. I stop thinking,
swim in silence and the truth comes to me.
-Albert Einstein

One of my acting teachers was the legendary Robert Lewis. An original Group Theater member, co-founder of The Actor's Studio and director of Broadway hits, he was filled with deep wisdom, experience, and knowledge. He was patient and gentle and he never lost his sense of humor. He was a master.

Bobby had us work on scenes in a unique way; he called it the "left page." We would make a copy of our script and then take each page individually and paste it onto a larger piece of paper and put them all in a binder. We had the text on the right and on the left, like an open book, was a blank page where we were to write our overall objective for the scene in one column and our actions to achieve that for each beat in another.

What I did, though, was to paste my script pages into a great big, oversized sketch book where each page was surrounded by a four-inch blank border which I then filled with notes written in tiny lettering. I was working on *The Corn is Green* and I'd read a biography of Montgomery Clift and discovered that Monty—who had also studied with Bobby—made notes in his script in the "character's" handwriting which, of course, I just had to emulate. I don't remember what I put down but I'm sure that it was exhaustive and penetrating and analytical and insightful and intellectual. You know. Real smart stuff.

We would sit at a small table in front of the class and talk through this work. Bobby would ask questions, occasionally standing up to expound on a point. The day I presented, Bobby spied my enormous pad. He stood up and moseyed over. He looked down. He circled behind me. He peered even closer. He strolled off to the side, stopped, turned, and looked at me. He sighed. He said: "Fields," he called me Fields, "Fields, if you don't give up being the intellectual, you will never get anywhere. You will never have a career." And he just looked at me. I flushed. I blushed. I broke a sweat. Bobby sat back down. A part of me knew he was spot on; that all my head talk was actually distancing me from the work. I was terrified.

In school, I had been given data to memorize. When I spat it back, when I intellectualized and used big words, when I discussed theories that I had read about and quoted them, I was rewarded. I was told that I was insightful and smart and given approval. But that day, I suddenly knew deep down that Bobby was right. This wouldn't work. I was horrified because I wanted it—acting—so badly and I had been conditioned to think at the world; to try to comprehend things by using intellect. How could I learn how to act without it? Wasn't analysis understanding? How could I learn anything? How could I function?

The circumstances of a play are imaginary to us. We know nothing personally, experientially about them. My father was never murdered by my uncle who then married my mother; my sister didn't hide in her room playing with tiny animal figurines made of glass. All imaginary to us, yet we habitually make assumptions about understanding the circumstances based on our intellect and ego that are neither specific nor personal and we accept them as true because we've been conditioned to believe what's "smart."

I believe that what I think is who I am and I splash that "me" over the work, well, actually over everything. But it isn't who I am and dragging the circumstances of the play to me is a disservice. And what if we don't have to be smart? What if it isn't about me? What if that "me" doesn't matter at all?

To truly be of service to the play, we need to start with and accept that we know nothing about these people, where they live, what they've gone through, what they do, and how they feel. It's all unknown, all imaginary to us. So, recognizing that, how do we close that gap?

*   *   *

Bernie Roshi Glassman trained under Taizan Maezumi Roshi at the Zen Center of Los Angeles in the '60s and '70s. After receiving dharma transmission from him, he established the Zen Community of New York and later the Greyston Mandala in Yonkers. In 1996, he founded the Zen Peacemakers where the Pure Precepts of Zen evolved into the Three Tenets of the Zen Peacemakers that Roshi Bernie articulated as:

Not Knowing
Bearing Witness
Taking Action

Not-knowing, in this Zen sense, is a place of profound silence and emptiness where ego and self-interest have not yet entered. Aspiring to be an empty vessel; one strives to be open to everything and refuse nothing. Not-knowing is entering a situation without being attached to any opinion, idea, or concept. Quiet. A quiet mind. Open to receiving everything that comes to us from all directions. Not-Knowing is giving up our fixed ideas about ourselves and the universe.

What a wonderful way to approach a script! Can we consider a script without any fixed ideas? Can we allow ourselves to let it wash over us while suspending our judgment and opinions? The Zen master Kosho Uchiyama had a phrase: "Open the hand of thought."[2] He meant that when we think, we're grasping something in the brain's conceptual fist. What if we were to just open that fist when we read the play and instead of flinging opinion and reason at it, let ourselves know nothing; what if we were to approach the script "not-knowing?" What would that be like?

The first exposure to a script is a special occasion—sacred, in fact. We should encounter it quietly. No coffee shop or gym or music or in the kitchen with the roommate. Settle into the big chair or on the bed or couch. Create a peaceful space to meet the play. Try to read it in one sitting. Let it be a gentle ritual.

We approach softly and humbly, and we invite it in; a delicate exchange. Like a musician sight-reading through a piece of music for the very first time: patient, absorbed, reverent. The notes. The rhythms and tempo. All about discovery; allowing themselves to be exposed to it freshly. No

---

[2] *Opening the Hand of Thought*. P.28 Kosho Uchimaya, translated and edited by Tom Wright, Jisho Warner, and Shoaku Okumura. Wisdom Publications.

thought. No analysis. No conclusions. These notes on that page: how do they feel in the fingers? How do they sound on top of and next to each other? How do they resonate in the body?

Then? Write down everything; your associations, memories, colors, images, impressions —everything. Respect all that arises. Treat them like a dream. When we dream, we don't dismiss what comes to us. We innately understand that every element has a personal significance. So too, anything that arises when we read a play has a personal meaning.

Karen Horney, the renowned psychoanalyst, instructed her students to always schedule a free hour after their initial session with a new patient. She had them use that time to write down each and every impression, association, and response that they had about the patient. Then she told them to put away their notes. A year later, after having worked with the patient in question, the student would revisit their initial observations and invariably, they would notice insights that were deeply relevant to the patient's situation; all their observations and suppositions would have come true!

Horney challenged her students to respond instinctively to their patient. What if we give ourselves permission to respond to the play in this way with no ego-driven critical mind.

We are conditioned to lead with our opinions; to jump in quickly with what we think. Or to worry about our "part." (How many of us say our lines aloud as we read the play for the first time?) What if I don't hold my response captive to my intellect and allow myself to Not Know?

I was a precocious and serious student of the classical guitar. When I was twelve, it came time for me to seek out "the" teacher. My parents and I found him: Alexander Bellow. A small, trim Russian, living on West 72nd street in Manhattan. He was renowned. I was to come with my music and my mother. He would see if he would take me on.

His living room was large and bright with big windows. Two chairs with footstools. A music stand. A guitar laying in an open case on a bench. A Velazquez! An amazing guitar: the Steinway of guitars.

After introductions, Mr. Bellow asked me to play a piece. I played something Spanish and showy with what I thought was great flair. He nodded. He shuffled through my music, pulled out something from the Renaissance and put it on the stand. I played. He nodded. He then asked me to play a C scale. I was surprised. Hadn't I just played two demanding pieces. Why would he want that?

I played the scale.

He nodded. A long pause. He looked at me. He said that he would teach me. He expected me to practice every day for at least an hour and this week I was to practice the C scale. I was thrilled to become his student. I had absolutely no idea what he meant or wanted from me with the scale, but I went home and played it. Again and again. Over and over. With ease. With speed. With flash. Every day. It was so easy.

Around the fourth day of this, though, something happened.

There I was, flying away—C up to C and back down again—when I stopped dead. A realization had come to me: I hadn't really been playing the scale! *What!?* No. *Yes!* It was a revelation. I felt it; it was true. What had I been doing then? I played the first note, the C.

Wait! No... *What?*

I played it again. This time, feeling it; in my fingers, in the middle of it. Just the solitary C. No "watch this" or "this is so easy."

I was *experiencing* it.

I moved slowly on to D.

It was amazing!

Then E...F...and so on...each note...up to C and back down again.

Each note.

Just like a breath.

I was hearing each note as if for the first time. And I was also hearing the space in between the notes! I was aware of the size and shape of the sound. I was wanting each of the notes and spaces to be equal. Somehow, I was inside it. And it was exquisite.

This, I have realized, is where we want to be when we, as actors, read a script. Deep, quiet and focused concentration. Just the play. Not-knowing. No me. Just receiving it; critical thought suspended. Accepting it.

In Zen, we talk about "dualistic" thinking in which I'm the subject and the world is the object that is outside of me. I slap my opinions on those objects seeing them as good or bad, right or wrong, black or white. I don't like him. I like her. That's bad. This is right.

I do this all the time without noticing that I'm doing it. This causes a certain suffering because whatever it is, is what it is, regardless of my opinion or what I want it to be. I am truly powerless over it or them. It's going to do and be whatever it is no matter what I want.

In Zen, we don't say "bad Harvey Weinstein" or "good Harvey Weinstein," we just say "Harvey Weinstein." That's him. And Harvey Weinstein does what Harvey Weinstein does; he Harvey Weinsteins. If I acknowledge that and accept it, no matter how vile I consider his behavior, it relieves me somewhat of my outrage and I can move in a constructive direction. This is tough. Weinstein hurt people, he caused harm, and we're asking ourselves to accept that? Yes, even when there is someone in the boat, there is never anyone in the boat.

What's more, there is no inside and outside, no subject and object, we are all of us inside together. Weinstein, Caitlin Clark, the Dalai Lama—all of us, everyone is in here and what I think about them is not them. It is only what I think and they are not my opinion of them. Also: I am not what I think!

I always identified with my thoughts. What I thought was who I was and the fancier my thoughts, the fancier I was. I equated self-esteem with my thinking. But they are just thoughts. They are not who I am, and they are not the truth just because I think them. In fact, when I impose them on something or someone, what I'm actually doing is applying my ego at the expense of what really is. So how about I just read that play as humbly and gently as possible?

"Good play" or "bad play" doesn't get me closer to its essence or a personal response. What happens if we dispense with our liking and disliking? Or judging my character in the play? Or thinking that I have to "make it work" or do it in a certain way so I'll be liked?

What if I allow the play to be the play and let it do what it does?

If I don't know, if I let it wash over me, do I see a color or images? What do I hear? Is it a noise, a piece of music, a song? And where does it take me? Memories surface and speak to me. What am I feeling? Where do those feelings live in my body?

When we allow this to happen; when we suspend our critical thinking and are still and alone with the script it will find a home in us. And when that happens, we've arrived at the second tenet: Bearing Witness.

After Not Knowing, Bearing Witness is inevitable. The practice of Bearing Witness is to give ourselves over to the joy and suffering that we encounter, to all the aspects of a situation. Rather than observing the situation, we strive to *become* the situation. When we Bear Witness, we become intimate with whatever it is: disease, delight, poverty, abundance, life itself, death itself.

Bearing Witness steers us to the moment and gives birth to the insight that comes from being present. We listen with our being. As Stella Adler would tell us, we listen with our blood. Our Not Knowing has expanded into Bearing Witness, and in Bearing Witness we become one with.

So let rehearsal be our Bearing Witness. By surrendering to the text, our partners, and the circumstances, we become intimate with the play; we can become one with it. If we take nothing for granted, then the circumstances really are "imaginary" to us, and everything becomes discovery.

So many times, I haven't seen the forest for the trees because I slid into loose, premature thinking about "my character." Or assumed an understanding of the circumstances. Assume nothing. Ask: what do we have to go on? What literally happens? What has the writer given us? What do the people in the play *do*? Why do they do what they do?

Consider David Rabe's *Hurlyburly*: A man sleeps with the woman his best friend has a crush on. A teenage runaway allows herself to be passed around like a bag of potato chips. Someone throws a woman out of their car while it's still moving while yet another snorts cocaine nonstop. These are irresponsible, destructive actions and it's very easy to be repelled by these people, to label them, to condemn them.

When we do that, we create distance. We're putting ourselves outside of them and falling into the trap of commenting on them. What happens, though, if instead of judging them and superficially illustrating that judgment, we Bear Witness? What happens if we ask, *Who behaves like this? What would be in me that I would do such things?*

Bear Witness and sit in what comes and you will arrive at what Mr. Rabe's play is about: pain, anguish, spiritual existential confusion. That's the "*Hurlyburly.*" That's where that behavior comes from; that's what I must find in myself to *be* in that play. Now I'm no longer watching, I'm inside.

Have I experienced those things? Yes? Do I understand them emotionally? Absolutely, yes. We all do. Now I'm in a position to use myself personally in the acting.

It is not my job to make the script work or make my character interesting. A violinist in the L.A. Phil doesn't feel compelled to "solve" Beethoven or Stravinsky. They're part of a section that's guided by the conductor. They don't interrupt the rehearsal to say they think that if they play with their bow upside down using the wood to hit the strings it will make Brahms more interesting.

No.

We get out of the way. We surrender as completely as possible. We give up thought. This can be difficult because we're dispensing with being intellectual. It's hard because it's not about us.

When we map out a performance based on analysis and then show that to the audience, that's about me. It's illustrative. What I'm doing is commenting on who I think the character is and what I think the play is about. Pfui.

It's seductive as well because I get to control the whole thing from my head. It comes from thinking that I must solve it or make it interesting. It caters to my ego because I've been conditioned to get attention and approval by being right. I'm caught up in wanting to be good. What is "good" anyway? It's what we want people to say about us;

he's a "good" actor. What is that? A parental pat on the head. And it's insidious. Without realizing it, our need for validation dictates what we do. Yes, it's nice to have, but it's beside the point. We don't do the work for that. We can't do the work for that. We do the work to do the work; we do the work for ourselves.

As Uta Hagen said, acting isn't something we churn out for public consumption. The feeling that comes when we are connected to the circumstances, in contact with our partners and living out the play moment to moment is so far beyond "good." It is fulfilling and affirming and has nothing to do with external praise.

*   *   *

Caymichael Patten was a director working in New York in the '70s and '80s. She was brilliant. She was tough. And I was her assistant. She was directing a fancy backer's reading and I asked to stage manage. She said sure, then told me that my job was to find out what she took in her coffee and to take her notes. She knew that I would want to put my two cents in, but I was to stay out of her way and under no circumstances was I to talk to the actors, especially R.A. Dow. She said to just watch him go about his business.

R.A. had been appearing all over town in shows by the hottest writers. I thought, because of what Cay had said, that he would be some kind of diva monster. Instead, there was this strikingly handsome, soft spoken, very sweet fellow. What was Cay on about? But then, something started to happen. R.A. would stop rehearsing, be silent for a moment, then quietly ask a question:

"How late is it?"

"Oh...He's my brother-in-law?"

"So, I knew her before?"

"We're in love?"

Simple. Specific. Basic. He allowed himself to know nothing about the circumstances. I remember thinking that his mind was like an L shaped corridor where every piece of the circumstances gathered one by one in the corner and he only let them pass through when they existed in him. It was a revelation seeing someone work so purely. He was patient and humble and he truly took nothing for granted. There is much talk in class and rehearsal about "intention," "action," "motivation." A student once asked acting teacher Freddie Kareman what his character "wanted" and Freddie shot back, "A ham sandwich—now just say the line." Those terms can be useful at a certain point but when we employ them early on, they are only abstractions and not based on any experience.

Analyzing away from rehearsal and predetermining a performance, I am literally outside the play and operating prematurely. I am "in my head." It's also very controlling. I decide what I'm going to do to "get what I want" without having experienced what the other characters are doing to me. I am excluding the actual living out of the moments; I am acting alone and it's all about me. It's a kind of manipulation that excludes vulnerability and the singular fragility that comes from human contact; the vital discovery that comes from interacting with others. It's like wearing blinders; I'm going to do what I'm going to do because this is what I do to get what I want regardless of what you may be doing. What brings me alive is what's between me and my partners and the sum of that, what's uncovered and created together in the moment is the magic and so very much larger than the parts. Wynn Handman would tell us that acting is what happens to you as you live out the moments! There was no muscle or noise in R.A.'s acting. By examining the "who, where, when, and what" without preconception or intellectualism, he was Bearing Witness. And when he did, his "acting" simply emerged.

Another word that's tossed around all the time is "organic" which can be defined as "characterized by continuous or natural development." What R.A. did was organic; it felt inevitable and truthful and personal, and he had, in fact, landed in the third tenet: Right Action.

Roshi Wendy Egyoku Nakao describes this as:

"Taking Action…The underlying intention is that the action that arises be a caring action, which serves everyone and everything, including yourself, in the whole situation. Sometimes the action is as simple as continuing on with the practice of the first two tenets of Not Knowing and Bearing Witness…And though the action that arises from the engagement of not-knowing and bearing witness is spontaneous and often surprising, it always fits the situation perfectly."[3]

So, in Bearing Witness we have personalized and gotten inside the circumstances and when we do that, the acting emerges. Our actions are inexorable; they feel reflexive and seem to come to us instinctively. They are right in front of us and we simply do them: Taking Action.

In Zen, we say that what we do, we do as fully as we can—whether it's chopping onions or open-heart surgery. When I asked Roshi Egyoku to be my teacher and she said yes and then I asked what I should do next, she replied, "The dishes." For a second I thought she was kidding but one look dispelled that notion. "Do the dishes" became Zen for me. Just like sitting down, standing up, laughing, crying, drinking, or eating; just doing the thing itself fully with no me, just the doing.

Shunryu Suzuki Roshi said:

---

[3] *Hold To the Center.* Tricycle. Summer 2017. P.39 Wendy Egyoku Nakao Roshi. Tricycle.Org.

"...when you do something, you should do it with your whole body and mind; you should be concentrated on what you do. You should do it completely like a good bonfire. You should not be a smoky fire. You should burn yourself completely."[4]

It wants to be the same with our acting; when that action surfaces, just do it. Throw yourself into it. No thought. No chat. No preciousness. No me. Everything is an opportunity to forget the self; to become what we are doing. When that happens, when I can leave me behind, it's astonishing.

---

[4] *Zen Mind, Beginner's Mind*. 1970. P.63. Shunryo Suzuki. Weatherhill.

2

JUST SAY THE LINE, JUST BREATHE

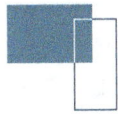

Since there is nothing but just this moment,
the time being is all the time there is.
-Eihei Dogen

Repetition is an acting training exercise created by Sanford Meisner that starts with a simple one sentence exchange between two partners and expands through the use of added elements into a scene. Meisner said that its goal is to get the actor to really listen, to really talk, and to really be in the moment. When I teach repetition, the first thing I do is to present Meisner's definition of acting:

Acting is behaving truthfully under imaginary circumstances.

I then ask for a volunteer to come up on stage. I ask them to jump and touch the ceiling. It's twelve feet to the ceiling in my studio. The volunteer usually gives me a curious look. I assure them that it isn't a trick and then ask them to go ahead and jump and try to touch the ceiling and to please keep doing it until I say stop. They go ahead and jump. At first, there may be some self-consciousness, but it dissolves as they give over to it. They find a rhythm. I have them go on for a while. They start to get breathless and maybe break a sweat. I stop them. I have them sit down. I ask them if they're okay; point out that they're breathing hard.

I then brag about my athletic prowess. I say I was an honorable mention All American in basketball in high school. I tell them they've never seen a middle-aged guy like me jump the way that I'm about to jump. Sometimes I wink at them, I might do a silly stretch, and then with one finger pointed daintily upward I hop about an inch off the floor. They don't know what's going on. I do it again. I look at them. "What did I just do?" I ask.

Someone might say, "You jumped."

Someone asks it as a question, "You jumped?"

"Really?" I speak. "Did I really jump?" I ask.

Looks all around.

Eventually, "No," someone answers.

"That's right," I say.

I tell them that I lied about the basketball stuff. I boasted and fooled around and flirted a bit, but I didn't really jump, did I? I point out that the volunteer got winded, that they were about to break a sweat. I then ask the volunteer if they worried about jumping "right" or jumping "good?" Were they concerned with how they looked; did they wonder if they were sexy? There's laughter. They always say no. I ask them what they were focused on. They say the ceiling. I ask the class did the volunteer really jump and try to touch the ceiling? Yes. Did I really jump? No!

I tell them again that acting is behaving truthfully under imaginary circumstances and add that the basis of truth in acting is the reality of doing. That whatever it is that we do, we REALLY do! We don't kind of do it; we don't sort of do it; we don't talk about doing it, we REALLY REALLY do it. With all of ourselves.

The student really jumped and focused on touching the ceiling. That's it. There it is. They gave over to doing it as fully as they could and burned themselves out just like Suzuki Roshi's bonfire.

I tell them that jumping at the ceiling is the ideal model for acting; that each jump is exactly like a moment in a play and that we live out that moment as fully as the student jumped. We pursue each one wholeheartedly to satisfy what each one demands. No two moments are identical. No two jumps were identical. Each was unique. Each moment is unique with its own unique size and shape and requirement.

I then ask the class if they think it took courage for our volunteer to come up in front of a group of strangers and follow my instructions regardless of how silly or difficult they may have been; to try to do the impossible, to touch the out-of-reach ceiling? Was that brave? Yes, they always answer. I affirm that: You bet. Damn straight. To put oneself at the disposal of a play and the character; to expose oneself physically and emotionally, to be willing to be sloppy and uncertain; to go to the bottom of who we are in the pursuit of the truth takes enormous courage. Roshi Egyoku said that Maezumi Roshi, referring to Zen practice, would say: "Have good guts!"

I ask them what they think technique is? This one is intimidating. Technique is one of them big words. The responses are hesitant; they're thinking they need to be profound. I tell them that technique is simply one's habits of work. Nothing fancy or English or deep. Nothing more, nothing less. Just your habits. Athletes and musicians and dancers have fabulous techniques. They show up and suit up and practice. (That's also what we call our meditation; a "meditation practice" where we sit over and over again.)

A wonderful example of technique is a baseball player at bat. That player has practiced their stance literally hundreds of thousands of times since they were little. It's in their body; in their muscles. Habit. If they feel tense or realize that they're thinking, they step out of the batter's box and take a breath, maybe roll their shoulders. They step back in and they focus on the pitcher; only watching for the "release point" of the ball coming out of the hand. If they're thinking: "I have to hit a home run and win the game," they're in trouble. They're in their head. The pitch will be past them before they know it. No. That stance is in them. They breathe and concentrate; alive and aware. See the ball. Hit the ball.

I ask, does the term "special self" resonate with them? There are tentative nods. I tell them that our special self is our brave, aware, vulnerable, human self. Make it our habit, I say, to bring our "special self" when we go to work; whenever we rehearse or step on stage, make it a part of our technique, our habit; it is essential to our ability to carry on.

After the jumping and the questions and the emphasizing that what we do we really do, I ask for another volunteer. I ask them if they can really listen. They usually say yes. I ask them to come up on stage and I put them about a dozen feet across from me and have them face me. I ask them to put their attention on me and to please leave themselves alone. I face them. There is an old Zen story: A student said to Master Ichu, "Please write for me something of great wisdom." Master Ichu picked up his brush and wrote one word: "Attention." The student said, "Is that all?" The Master wrote, "Attention. Attention." The student became irritable, "That doesn't seem profound or subtle to me." In response, Master Ichu wrote simply, "Attention. Attention. Attention." In frustration, the student demanded, "What does this word attention mean?" Master Ichu replied, "Attention means attention." I tell the student across from me that I want them to place their attention on me and really listen and to repeat as accurately as possible what they might hear. I then make a simple observation about something that literally exists on them. "Your shirt is blue." "You're wearing leggings." "Your collar is buttoned." And they repeat it. And then I repeat it. And then they repeat it. And there we are: we have started repetition, Sanford Meisner's extraordinary training exercise. Every class, we add new elements—"independent " physical activities, the meaning of the relationship, the moment before, emotional preparation—until it builds into a scene. And the basis of it all is being in the moment with the partner; really listening and really responding.

We emphasize over and over again:

Leave yourself alone.

Put your attention on the partner.

Each moment is new.

Each moment is different.

Put your gentle attention on your partner.

You never know what's coming next.

Leave yourself alone.

When in doubt, repeat.

Act before you think.

The partner is the most important person on stage.

Put your gentle human attention on your partner.

What you do doesn't depend on you, it depends on the partner. When you're pinched, you "ouch."

Contact. Contact. Contact.

Gentle human contact.

Leave yourself alone.

We train ourselves to give over to the partner and the moment; to leave ourselves behind and to live it out. By acting before we think, we act from our instincts and as I build this habit of throwing myself into the moment, I create the practice of using more and more of myself, of putting myself at the disposal of the play without any thinking or manipulation. It becomes our technique, and we learn to leave who we think we have to be, or what we think we need to do, to be a "good" actor, behind.

*　　　　*　　　　*

In Zen, we sit "zazen", which literally means "sitting Zen." Zen meditation: I cross my legs in a certain posture making sure I'm stable. I place my left hand palm up on top of the palm of my right hand, gently touching my thumb tips together and then place them in my lap against my lower belly. I look at the floor in front of me with softly focused eyes and let my breath drop down into a spot below my belly button. I breathe in and then count that breath internally on the exhalation until I reach ten and then go back to one. Inhale, exhale, "one." Inhale, exhale, "two," and so on until ten. Counting the breath develops our concentration and settles our body. It guides us to being right here, right now. In his book, *Appreciate Your Life*, Maezumi Roshi says: "By following the breath, you reduce it to...inhalation and exhalation. But it is not simply a matter of two, ten, or one hundred. Don't forget, breathing is life. By breathing genuinely in this way, you begin to live in this way. In what way? You appreciate the life that you are living *in this very moment*."[5]

One time I was pruning a climbing rose that I had trained to grow up a drainpipe in front of my house. Standing tiptoe on an old stump, I was reaching up when suddenly the stump came apart under me and I fell into the rose. The thorns and vines grabbed my clothing—luckily, I was wearing a sweatshirt and long pants—and I found myself

---

[5] *Appreciate Your Life*. P.164 Taizan Maezumi Roshi. Shambhala.

good and stuck. I couldn't move and I was suddenly aware of being right there in that very moment trapped by the vine. Nothing else. I was present as if for the very first time. I was amazed! Where had I been before? Where was I when I'd been snipping away? Where was I when I was cooking or driving or being with my kids? Did I really live in my head that much?

I'd been slammed into the present and the gap between all my thinking and being here right now was distinct and palpable! Falling into the rose, I was confronted with how I separated myself from my life with my thinking.

In acting, too, we want to eliminate separation. We try to do away with thinking by giving over to the moment which is the same as following the breath in meditation. I am not present, though, when I fall into watching and judging—there's a Zen saying: *you don't need another head on top of your head*—when I'm deciding that this is how it should go or this is bad. That's how I invalidate what I'm experiencing in that very moment. I'm in service to some "should" that is just a notion to satisfy my ego. And I'm incessantly trying to satisfy that " should" which leads to constant evaluating which creates a separation that produces a kind of suffering because that separation can never be mended.

Likewise, sitting there in meditation, a memory or a concern surfaces; we grab it and go spinning away into thought. Eventually, though, we realize that we've traveled somewhere and so we come back. We wake up to these patterns that function within us and when we find that we've been carried away, we return to the breath—simply go back to one and start again. Yet, here's the thing: we're usually unkind to ourselves about this: we're not doing it right; we're "bad" meditators; there's something wrong with us. That's pretty much a reflex; thinking that we have to hit a bull's eye or it's just no good. But by just returning, we learn to be kind to ourselves. We come to understand that the going away and coming back happens; it's a part of it and we forgive ourselves. The more I have the experience of knowing the effect of this choice—the intention to return—the stronger my ability to return becomes. We're building our focused attention like a muscle we're training. My inner narrative quiets down and my critical self-consciousness lessens. When we wander, we just return to this breath and body, to this moment right now. Roshi Egyoku said that returning to the breath is a major event in our lives; this continual returning is indeed an awakening. We come to accept that this is the way our mind works, and we begin to be gentle with ourselves and to become confident in our coming back. That is what the practice is. Spaciousness and gentle awareness, a certain kind acceptance that comes with meditation. The clinging to thoughts and patterns dissolves. Uchiyama Roshi said that thoughts are only the secretions of the mind. They are just what our mind does and it's fine. They are only thoughts, and they are a part of it. Just come back.

In repetition, we teach ourselves the same thing. I am going to wander for sure—it's human—but I leave myself alone and come back. This happens all the time in our acting as well. We're on stage and we realize that we're wondering where we're going to go to eat after the show or that we hate our costume or why is that person in the first row jiggling their foot and we just come back. We put our attention on the partner and listen. When we go to our head; discover ourselves outside and above, watching and listening, finding fault and judging, we return to the partner and the moment; to always come back; to leave ourselves and our thinking behind. In acting, I pursue the moment. In meditation, I follow the breath. They are exactly the same. Like jumping at the ceiling, we strive to live out each moment as completely as each moment demands giving over to each of them fully. Each is unique: they have their own integrity: size, shape, quality that we try to realize. They are like a string of pearls running away into the distance that we move forward with; that is the play arising in front of us; there is our Right Action. This moment and then this moment and then this moment and then this moment. Like my playing that C scale for Mr. Bellow.

Meditating, we breathe and then there is the next breath and the next breath and the next breath and the next breath. This one. This one. This one. This one. Following the breath takes concentrated effort and the more we practice the more easily it comes to us.

By doing this, we get the mind to sit, to quiet, which allows us to be present right here right now. Maezumi Roshi said: "When I was in college...I studied with Koryu Roshi. Koryu Roshi often said, 'When you breathe in, breathe in the whole universe. When you breathe out, breathe out the whole universe. Breathing in and out, in and out, eventually you even forget who is breathing what.' There is not inside, no outside; no this, no that. Everything all together is disappearing. So, what is there? You can answer, 'Nothing.' When you truly sit, you can also say, 'Everything.'"[6]

And like returning to the breath after having floated into thought during meditation, the actor returns continually to the partner and the next moment. And like the Zen practitioner, we come to understand that that moment is all there is—it is the past, the present, and the future, it is everything.

Listening like a sponge is called absorptive listening. I soak up what others are saying and let the mind be quiet without formulating a response until a response is required. Ideal for acting: I

[6] *Appreciate Your Life*. P.164 Taizan Maezumi Roshi. Shambhala.

forget myself and put all my attention on you, absorbing what you're saying.

There is a Buddhist recitation for invoking compassion: "We should practice listening so attentively that we are able to hear what the other is saying—and also, what is left unsaid. We know that by listening deeply we already alleviate a great deal of pain and suffering in the other."[7]

We really listen: To the play. To the partner. To the moment. All I actually "have" is the moment and to give over to it completely by listening is to connect with it. Being vulnerable isn't about crying, it's allowing ourselves to be penetrable "off" the partner; everything "does" us. Freddie Kareman would tell us to be as flexible as a blade of grass in the breeze.

When I'm connected, the behavior and words flow out of me dictated by my contact with the partner and my acting comes from my gut, my instincts. I am "using" myself. We say in repetition: "What you do doesn't depend on you, it depends on the other guy." That the acting is in the response; you're "pinching" me and I'm "ouching." The tenet of Bearing Witness came out of the Zen precept of Deep Listening and responding to the partner is the Right Action and that is the play!

In Zen, we join our hands palm to palm sealed together. It's called "Gassho." One. One with. Both sides together. No separation. We say,

---

[7] *How to Train an Elephant to Dance.* P.160 Jan Chozen Bays. Shambhala.

"Let the heat kill you. Let the cold kill you." Be the heat. Be the cold. No me here and heat there that's bothering this me. No me, only heat. Close the gap, no separation. Gassho. Being one with Buddha. Being one with driving to work or cleaning the tub. When I meditate and the leaf blower is grinding away outside, it's not leaf blower annoying me; there's no "me" to be annoyed. I become one with the sound; I am the sound and we are together right here right now.

So too with my acting: be one with the moment; there is only the response that is dictated by connection. There is no me over here watching you over there and commenting on you or me or the scene. No self-manipulation based on that. No showing what we think the play is about or who we think our character is or "playing" some strategy to achieve an intention. No. No separation. One with the partner, one with the moment.

*   *   *

When we start to meditate, though, we are usually not situated in the oneness of life but in the sense of being separate and in the dualistic thinking that comes with that separation; good/bad, right/ wrong.

That sense of separation and the black/ white-ness of the world is called delusion. It is me as subject and you as object. Me over here and you over there. The divide between us is filled with ego and craving and it causes suffering. But there is no you outside. And no me inside. And what's more, there's no inside or outside to begin with. There's just all of us together inside an infinite circle.

With acting the delusion was in my constant thinking about myself. I was less than, lacking; I wasn't going to be able to "get there." I wasn't doing enough; there was something that I needed to do—had no idea what it was—but I wasn't doing it.

I'd be rehearsing or in class and I'd find myself angry. Something was wrong somewhere and it was somebody's fault. When things weren't perfect or didn't happen effortlessly, I would punish myself and the tension and anger would spill over into the work. The fear, the negativity, the competitiveness, all the "self" stuff—self-consciousness, self-contempt, self-laceration, self-doubt—was reflexive and unconscious. It was a familiar companion that I could rely on in a perverse way. It was safe because it was predictable: it also hijacked the work forcing me to be lost in the result with the only escape being to hit that bull's-eye.

This was my Hungry Ghost. In Zen, we talk about having a Hungry Ghost. It's pictured as a forlorn figure with an enormous gaping mouth, elongated neck and a bloated stomach. It's the voracious thing that wants and wants and wants.

Never satisfied. Starving. Always hungry for more. For me, it was about attaining acknowledgement and affirmation, attention and praise, recognition, and love. Always whirring away just beneath the surface, it was insatiable and destructive; insinuating itself into everything which, of course, included my acting. In fact, it frequently took my acting hostage. The work became about everyone loving me—yes, I appreciate that that's a cliché, but it was true—and the only way to attain that love was to be "perfect" and then all the pain and loneliness and desperation that I lived in because I wasn't "perfect" would disappear. And the love would make me "perfect." And I would be saved. But the only way to get the love that would make me "perfect" was to be "perfect." Except, I was never going to be "perfect!" A crippling burden, an agonizing Catch-22, and a true prescription for suffering.

So, if I was never going to get saved because I was never going to be good enough; never be loved because I would never be perfect, what could I do? Answer? The work.

I can do "the work." No matter what. Everyday. Just like zazen. Practice. No one can really teach anyone to act. It's like music. I can't make anyone musical. No amount of theory or talk or technical instruction can do that. I can show you how to hold your hands and place your fingers, but I can't make you expressive. Note perfect fast fingers don't add up to being musical. It is constant practice and playing that gets you to the music that is in you—and what that is, who really knows? I do know, though, that it comes forth as you give over to the playing. It's the same with acting. You go to class to get down to the acting that's in you, and when you start to live there and work from there really using yourself, we say it's acting. We don't really know what it is, but we know it's acting.

With zazen we are told to just sit there and breathe. We're not trying to change our mood or bliss out; the instruction is to drop off body and mind and sit. We are also told that as we sit, we will meet our true self. With all of it: acting, music, mediation, it is the doing, the over and over again, the dogged perseverance, the process, not the product, that is all. Yes, the small ego-ridden self will be there waiting and wanting. Yes, the Hungry Ghost will grasp. That's fine. Invite them to do the work with you.

Actors freak out when they're nervous; they get frightened. They think that something's wrong because they're nervous. There's nothing wrong: I'm just nervous. Aren't we supposed to be nervous? You can't shove the nerves away. You can't trick yourself about them. They're there whether we like it or not. No, let them be there, even invite them in.

Roshi Egyoku had me make a little sculpture of my Hungry Ghost and place it where I meditate and to give it an offering, to feed it, every day. She also told me to invite it to sit next to me while I meditated. And my relationship to it changed. I experienced the hurt and fear that made me need so much. And it wasn't an "it" outside of me anymore, but me. My hurt, my fear, my need; and the opportunity, the obligation, to sooth and forgive myself, arose.

Bernie Roshi Glassman wrote:

"There is a little toy called a Chinese finger trap: You put two fingers into it, then try to pull them out. But you can't extricate your fingers by pulling; it's only when you push your fingers further in that the trap releases them. Similarly, we think of letting go as doing something: throwing things away...But that works no better than pulling our fingers in order to extricate them from the trap. We let go by eliminating the separation between us and what we wish to let go of. We *become* it."[8]

My Hungry Ghost is me. My nerves and doubt and insecurities are me. All my self-involvement is me. I need to accept and befriend all of it in the same way that I come back to my breath or return to the moment. With compassion. I must learn to forgive myself.

I often ask a student if they intend on being a parent. When they say yes, I ask them if they'll yell at their child when the child doesn't understand something? They respond, of course not. I ask the

---

[8] *Infinite Circle: Teachings in Zen.* P.67 Bernie Glassman. Shambhala.

class what is that, screaming at a child when they don't get it? They answer: abuse. I say absolutely and we don't treat a child that way. I then tell them that that child is the actor in them, that they have to be as gentle with themselves as they would be with their child. So, no bad actor or bad Buddhist; we're all in here and everything is okay. And I keep going; I do the work. The work is what saves me because like meditation it leads me to my true best self, because the work is ultimately an act of compassion, it is love.

The Avatamsaka Sutra says, "Great Compassion is the essence of meditation. It is her body, her source and her means to spread herself through the whole universe. Without this 'great heart' of love and compassion, meditation, however sublime it may be in other respects, is of absolutely no value."

*   *   *

Once, I went into dokusan—the private one-to-one interview with a teacher—with Sensei Faith Mind Thoresen, and I said, with false modesty, about my meditating, "I'm just this guy. Just this guy who is sitting there breathing." Immediately she responded "NO! NO GUY! ONLY BREATHING. ONLY THE BREATH. NO GUY!" Many times I've sat next to a playwright during rehearsal and they would whisper in response to what an actor was doing, "Say the line." Then, "Just say the line!" And then, "Tell them to just say the line!!!" Really that simple. We do not have to make it work.

We think that in some way, we are responsible for the play. We say, "I have to do the play tonight," or "I have to do a scene in class." Nope. I don't "do" the play; the play "does" me. It's not mine to do or improve upon. That play is going to happen at 8:00pm tonight and it is my privilege to enter into it; to let it "do" me. The moment is "doing" us. The play is "doing" us. No thought. No muscle.

Dōgen Zenji, the "father" of Soto Zen, said: "Scrubbed clean by the dawn wind, the night mist clears. Dimly seen, the blue mountains form a single line." This being "scrubbed clean by the dawn wind" is not only about a time of day, but also about the freshness available in each breath. And "the night mist clears" is the process of bringing myself back to attention and awareness, realizing, waking up. The moment.

In acting, it is the coming back to the partner and the moment. Inhaling the moment. "Dimly seen the blue mountains form a line." These mountains are the events, the issues and the problems of our lives. They are also each moment in the play forming a line—the progression of the story and the actions of my character. Live each moment of our lives as fully as we can. Live each moment of the script as fully as we can.

Towards the conclusion of repetition training, we do what we call the "First Scene." We have been practicing listening and repeating, listening and responding, "working off" the other guy, again and again, over and over, moment to moment to moment. We've built these acting muscles; we're now capable of staying present and penetrable and returning to the moment. We are given a short scene of two to three pages. No one is screaming or throwing things or going through an emotional catharsis. It's a simple scene and we're to memorize it technically. Just learn the words cold; get command of the text.

We're then instructed to repeat with our partner and to let the scene come out of the repetition; to let the first line just come out arbitrarily and then the partner responds with their line and then to go back and forth with the text.

At first, it's awkward and mechanical, but as we give over, respond with our line and are "pinched" by the partner with their line and go moment to moment, line to line, we begin to express the words sans thought or manipulation. The acting is the response dictated by what the other guy is doing to us and the text is there to articulate it.

The first time I did this, after the initial awkwardness, I found myself beyond not thinking and not watching myself and it was an incredible relief. This I could do; I felt for the first time that I would be able to act. It was as if I was floating; you can't deny the experience of inhabiting each moment.

Acting before thinking!

Just this moment.

And then this moment.

And then this moment.

Like really really playing each note.

Like each breath in zazen.

Like Dōgen's blue mountains!

It is all just these moments and my job is to get myself out of the way and to serve them; to be a conduit. When we live them out, that is the action of the play. That is how the story is told and we are its servants.

*   *   *

I'm in the movie Jurassic Park. The location was in Red Rock Canyon in the Mojave Desert. There were buttes in the distance, cactus in the little valleys and because it was a California condor preserve, park rangers ranged to make sure we didn't stray off the marked paths. It was otherworldly, eerie, beautiful, and incredibly hot.

The first day, first thing, I was sent to wardrobe. I was wearing jeans and canvas sneakers and a green short-sleeved shirt I'd gotten in Connecticut the week before.

I climbed the stairs into the wardrobe trailer where I introduced myself to the two women who were sitting there chatting. They reminded me of my aunt Rose; I wouldn't have been surprised if they asked me, did I want something to eat? They smiled; they were calm; they were sweet. Then Sue, the designer, stood up, stepped closer and walked around me. She stepped back and studied me a bit more, then said, "What you have on works. Just wear that."

I didn't know what to say. I had expected to have to try on all sorts of pants and shirts and shoes with endless scrutinizing and discussion. Instead, I'd been in there for all of five minutes. They sent me on my way to hair and makeup.

Inside that trailer there was an old man wearing an enormous straw hat—the kind you'd wear to the beach. He introduced himself: Monte. Monte had to be in his late 70s. The hair and makeup trailers that I'd been in always bustled with banter and music and people coming and going and the chatter and static of walkie-talkies but here it was just me and Monte.

Monte pointed to a chair and I sat. We exchanged "Hi's." He looked at me in the mirror. Then he swiveled the chair so he could look straight at me. Then he swiveled me back. He softly dusted my forehead and cheeks and nose with some powder then he brushed them with his fingers. He tousled my hair and pushed my bangs to the side and said, "That's fine. You're good to go."

Again, all of five minutes. Again, no fuss. No pancake batter makeup or greasy eyeliner. He sent me on to set. I did my first scene where I walked up the hill and called out my line and that was that.

The next day, after a Monte look and pat, was me displaying an image of velociraptor bones on my computer screen and doing a bit of show and tell. Steven Spielberg likes to shoot, to literally run the camera himself. He was sitting on the camera dolly about six feet away from me. I was thrilled. I was excited.

We did a take. Steven popped his head away from the camera's eyepiece and leaned forward and, so no one else could hear, he said, "What you just did...you don't have to do all of that...don't do anything, okay?" Something clicked: look at the computer and just talk. I did that and after the take, Steven smiled and nodded.

The message was simple: it's enough just as it is. It's fine. You're fine. Go about your job with gratitude and humility.

Just say the line.

*   *   *

Living in Los Angeles, I realized, I'm from New York, that I missed riding on buses and the subway.

I yearned for all the people. Sitting there on the Broadway local, I could lower my book to my lap and take in all the people ranged in front of me. Dear. Scary. Silly. Old. Young. Like a feast. Each beautiful in their own way. All those lives right there; human, unique, humanly unique, uniquely human. Being captivated; wanting to know who they were and what it felt like to be them.

Stella Adler had an exercise: we would go to a museum, choose a painting with people in it and "get" one of them. Who were they? Where did they come from? Why were they there? What were they doing and why? What did it feel like to be them?! Get them! Be them! We would return to class where we would be them doing a simple task. It was challenging and Stella was extremely demanding, but when we stopped thinking and illustrating and allowed ourselves to just do, it was a revelation.

When my daughters were little, six and nine, we had a favorite diner where we'd go for the macaroni and cheese, milk shakes and the jukebox. While we waited for our food, listening to Creedence Clearwater Revival, we'd play the "restaurant game": we'd pick a table and give each of the people a biography: he's a poet from Chile who had to flee to the US and that's his third wife and the two teenage girls are his stepdaughters who go to Immaculate Heart which they hate. And on and on.

Empathy is a muscle that can be built, strengthened and maintained, like contact; like our return to the breath in meditation or coming back to the partner in a scene. You could say that contact is empathy and that empathy leads to compassion and loving kindness and we can build and practice those as well. Isn't that what our acting can be; understanding and kindness, a shared humanity? To be connected is to be compassionate is to be one with.

In his book *The Light Inside the Dark*, John Tarrant says, "Attention is the most basic form of love; through it we bless and are blessed."[9] It's like a door in my chest that I can open: riding the 104 bus, taking those people in, I would delight in them and experience affection—if not love for them, to connect to them.

In Zen, we say that we are connected to everyone and everything; we are all each other; we are all one; that subject and object are intrinsically one. Look up at the sky. Notice the trees. Feel the ground under your feet, the world, coming up into your body. Open your ears and really hear those sounds whirling around you. Present. Here. With everyone, all together. A part of. Not separate.

We can have that in our acting: gentle attention on the partner—whatever or whomever it is—and loving human connection with them and with every moment. One with.

---

[9] *The Light Inside the Dark*. P.6 John Tarrant. Harper Collins .

3

THE CHARACTER AND KOAN

I implore you...to have patience with everything that has not been resolved in your heart. Try to love <u>the questions</u> themselves...<u>Live</u> the questions...

-*Rainer Maria Rilke*

When I started out, I thought that "character" was lisping and limping, an artificial nose or an accent. Some external application to be displayed for effect, basically a physical condition. Then I saw Meryl Streep in Thomas Babe's *Taken in Marriage* and that was a whole other thing entirely.

What she was doing up there was so human and distinct and compelling and not about the exterior at all. I realized character was much more than what I had thought it was and that what I was doing was external. I needed to go deeper somehow.

I thought the answer was to talk myself into a character by dint of analytic observation—the very thing that Bobby Lewis had confronted me about—and that would magically transform me into this mysterious other. I slapped adjectives on like so much spackle: "He's aggressive. He's shy. He's obsessive." The next thing I knew, I'm trying out my shy voice or making my best obsessive faces. I fell right into the trap of showing the audience who I thought the character was by illustrating my opinions and adjectives. That is commenting and general and superficial. It was as though the character was some guy over there that wasn't me and by talking about him a whole lot, I'd become him.

We've all done it.

It's indicating.

And "indicating" is a dirty word in acting. Indicating comes from that place of having to be smart for effect, where we are enamored with our "insights" which are for the most part general and external. The character is not a "he" or "she" to be talked about; that is "third person" acting. There is no guy or gal over there! I am the guy! No third person, always first person.

Framing this through a Zen lens? What I was doing was residing in dualistic thinking. There's a subject, me here, and an object, the character over there, and I look to "become" that object by exposing it to my discursive thinking. I attempt to navigate the separation that I've created by using the very thing that's created it: my thinking.

Only there is no subject/object.

There is no separation.

Subject and object are intrinsically one.

I am one with.

How can that happen; how do I do that? I have to be willing to Not-Know. It's essential to recognize and accept that we know nothing about the character or the play and we get ourselves into the weeds because we have to know; to "come up with something," be insightful, be a "good" actor etc... Nope.

Like letting the script wash over us, we give ourselves permission to not know, to open the hand of thought and humbly go moment to moment allowing what we experience to inform us. We become one with by doing, experiencing; by giving over, bravely, stupidly—like the repetition—diving headlong into the action.

Usually, though, my ego sees the discomfort of not-knowing as a bad thing. This anxiousness means there's something wrong; that I must be missing something. But I'm not. I just simply don't know yet. What we need to do is to welcome it; to lean into the doubt and frustration and awkwardness. How many times do we judge a character? We do that. We label them. Sometimes we dislike them or we "don't want to be seen that way,"- which, if you think about it, is massively self-centered! We might even get defensive as if the character is some sort of imposition. How often do we become churlish because we have to be "good" actors and we can't tolerate the frustration of not-knowing? When we realize that it is not about me and welcome the discomfort and see it as an opportunity, we become free to simply discover and do what the play requires.

*   *   *

Koans are a tool used by Zen teachers. They are apparently paradoxical statements or stories or questions designed to induce intense doubt in their students that allows them to cut through their conventional, conditioned thinking to see their true nature directly.

How do you stop the sound of the temple bell?

Show me an unmovable tree in the heavy wind.

Take Mount Everest out of your sleeve.

Working with a koan, I must go past trying to use logic to understand it to embodying it; to "become one with the koan." To become one with the sound of the temple bell, become the unmovable tree, to take the mountain out of my sleeve.

Wrestling and grappling with it is "becoming one with." That's how we become it. That's how we work with koans. That's how to work with the play—like R.A. Dow in rehearsal embracing what he didn't know and asking his simple questions about the circumstances.

When I taught workshops for teenagers, the first thing I would do is have them listen to the slow movement from Beethoven's Ninth Symphony. As it traveled and unraveled, bending time and weaving melody, the kids literally had no idea what they were hearing; what was this; when would it end? And then slowly and surely, it would grab them and go into them. When it finished, we would sit quietly for a bit and then I would ask: "What was that?"

They were speechless. What did I mean? What did I want?

I'd continue, "What was that about?"

Silence and bewildered looks.

"What did you see?"

Slowly they would begin to answer:

"The ocean."

"A sunset."

"Loneliness."

"Leaves."

"Someone walking in the woods."

"Childhood."

"The waves."

"Life."

59

"Love; two lovers."

"A river."

"Heartbreak."

"Death."

It would roll out of them.

I'd ask, "Where did that come from?"

Puzzlement. Furrowed brows.

Then, hesitantly, one would say, "From me?"

"Yes!" I'd say and then, "What is that?"

"Huh?"

"What is that?!"

"Me?"

"Yes! You. What is that?"

"Umm...myself?"

"Yes! You! Yourself! You! No one else. Each of you unique; only one of you. And what was it that you said?"

"What I saw...what I imagined."

"Yes! And...?"

"My...my...feelings?"

"Yes!! Your response to it. From you. No one else."

I'd ask, "Who knows music theory or composition? Harmony? Counterpoint?"

No one.

I'd point out that they didn't need technical know-how for what just happened; that at first they were stumped because they thought they had to have the right answer; what they thought I wanted them to say; something impressive and analytical. But then they went to a place, didn't they, that was beyond that, a non-thinking place, where they let the music "do" them, where they experienced the music and responded from who they are. I'd look at each of them in turn and say, "That's where your acting comes from. That place in you. You!"

Beethoven as koan.

In repetition, we say that the acting is in the response. And that response is, in fact, an emotional one. That's a huge word for actors: emotion. We immediately think it means crying. Crying and screaming and breaking things. I did. Most people think that acting is just that, crying. The joke goes: If acting was crying my mother would have been a big star.

No. Emotion is an underground river that runs in us continually. To be human and alive is to be emotional. I am very emotional as I type this. You're emotional as you read it. Everything is emotional. Not rending, gnashing, sobbing. It's not hysterical or histrionic. It's being alive and human, and it simply flows in us incessantly. That's where our responses come from. We're moved to tears by a song or sigh when we see something that's beautiful. That's how an actor "understands." Not from the head but from the gut. Emotional understanding: we are connected and responsive.

In the opening scene of Arthur Miller's *Death of a Salesman,* two brothers, Biff and Happy, are in their childhood bedroom preparing to go to sleep. They're grown men now. Biff has returned from being out west while Happy has his own place and is only staying there for the night. What are their emotional responses to this place; this room where they grew up; their home?

Biff: My father, Willy the salesman, fed me lies; when I needed him the most, I discovered him cheating on my mother; he betrayed my mother and me and he broke my heart. I fled the city and over the last few years have had twenty or thirty jobs while also doing some time in jail. I've come home because I realize that I've been wasting my life. The emotional meaning of home is my father's deception and what that did to me, heartbreak and failure.

Happy: My older brother, Biff, was a big star athlete in high school getting all the attention, especially dad's. It was Biff this and Biff that. I had to be his fan too; I carried his towel and cleaned up after him. His team pennants and trophies surrounded us. There was no room for me, literally and figuratively. How would you feel if all your parents' attention and love was given to your sibling? Me? I'd be desperate and jealous and angry. That's what home is to me.

So, I "understand" emotionally. I put myself in the circumstances and ask: "How does that make me feel? What does that do to me?" And having identified that, I examine how those feelings live in me and now the play is personal to me.

If I'm Blanche DuBois, I've been slowly coming apart ever since, as a young girl, I shamed my husband about his sexuality and he killed himself. I've been self-destructive and reckless and promiscuous. I lost the family home. Ultimately, I slept with an underage boy and was thrown out of town. I arrive at my sister and her husband's small sweaty apartment with nowhere else to go. My brother-in-law is predatory and hostile. What does this do to me; how does it make me feel; what is the emotional meaning of this place to me? I am trapped and terrified.

That Beethoven is a koan. It defies intellect. To "understand" it, I only need to let it wash over me; to breathe it in, to enter it. My "understanding" is in my response. Jackson Pollock, Balanchine, Anne Sexton: all koans. I don't have to know a thing about brush strokes or an arabesque or scansion to respond to what's in that canvas or choreography or poem.

I respond emotionally without thought, with no need for intellectual explanation. I respond from my self. When we work with a koan, we are relentless in our pursuit and application until we're saturated with it—it's embedded in me. No analysis; it's not a matter of discussion or explanation. I've experienced it and it is in me and I embody it. How do I stop the temple bell from ringing? I go past the snare of the impossible question to just being the bell. "Donnng."

Children are great with koans. Say to them, "Show me an unmovable tree in the heavy wind," and they'll stand there and be a tree. End of story. They don't suffer from the curse of having to be smart, they perceive what's alive and can express it freely.

When we wrestle with the character, it is exactly like wrestling with a koan. At first, there is the trap of believing that we have to figure it out; something to solve with thinking. When we do that, though, we create a gap. We place the character over there and talk at them, but keep in mind, the character isn't an amalgamation of adjectives that is standing over there outside of us, an object for discussion. It is not third person; it is first person. I. Me.

I cannot think myself into a character.

The character is right here, and I am the character just as I am the koan.

Biff is a koan. Happy is a koan. Blanche is a koan. No thought. No intellect. No discursive mind weighing, analyzing, worrying about the effect of what you're doing; wondering how you'll look or if they'll like you. No trying to get it "right," to "answer" some question. The key is to experience; to experience the koan and to experience the character BY DOING.

How do I pull a mountain out of my sleeve? Well...let me think about that...nope—no thinking. I pull it out and here it is and I give it to you. If I have to throw a chair, I don't have to think about it, I just throw the chair.

When I'm thoroughly engaged, I can't separate the koan from myself or myself from the koan. It has come alive in me; that's when we say that the koan is "turning" us; the koan is using me to understand what it is. Similarly with acting, if I leap into fully experiencing the moments, the character will come alive and find a home in me. The role manifests itself like the koan does and it's about what I'm doing versus what I think I should show you about who I think the character is.

What remains when we remove all the mind chatter is a puzzle I know nothing about: not-knowing. And not-knowing leads to bearing witness. With a koan, bearing witness is sitting in the confusion. Thinking isn't going to help. There's no escape; I have to dive into what I can't figure out. With acting, it is engaging my courage and throwing myself into the work and allowing it to be messy. It's permitting ourselves to accept the awkwardness of not-knowing while listening deeply to our insides as we live out the actions.

Once when I was working with Cay Patten, she stopped me and said, "You already got the part." I had been so wrapped up in needing everything to be right and neat and ready, having to be the "best" actor in the room that there was zero space for exploration or a revelatory mistake or just plain out-and-out practice—which rehearsal is, by the way, a lot of practice. I suffered from having to "know" right now and needing to "have it" immediately.

What I don't understand.

What I don't know.

What feels uncomfortable.

What I judge, dislike, condemn.

What I ignore and want to dismiss...

...is the vein of gold to mine! The riddle to welcome and unravel.

The line or moment that I just can't seem to comprehend and rebel against is the koan.

My vexation will guide me if I can stop thrashing around in my head and be still.

When a pianist first sits down to work on a piece, they're just trying to make out where their fingers need to go; they're starting a journey. They sight-read through it, listening and sensing it in their fingers and they know that as they learn it technically and get it into their hands and body, their instinctive response will surface and weave itself into their playing. That is "being musical." They are responding to what they're doing from deep within themselves; from who they are.

The great pianist Maurizio Pollini said he wouldn't perform a piece unless he had lived with it for two years, while the magnificent Yo Yo Ma said that he needs to have the music in his body before he plays it in public.

Piece of music as koan!

Character as koan!

After I'd worked and worked on a piece and was saturated in it, Mr. Bellow would take the music that was resting on the stand and turn it around, so its back was to me, smile a small smile and say, "Now make music."

Sanford Meisner said, "Prepare everything but the acting." When we can leave ourselves behind and give over to and express what is surfacing from the doing, there's the acting; it's what happens to us as we pursue the moments and that does not come from our head and we do not manipulate it. It's our human response arising before thought. Act before you think!

We're "making music." And we sense this, don't we? We do. It's when we're out there on stage and we don't know what the next moment is and we feel like we're making up the lines as we go. There's an effortlessness, a flow that is wildly fulfilling.

When we work to experience becoming one with the koan, we begin to perceive that, in fact, everything is a koan—arguing with my daughter or talking to customer service or going on a date—where the anger or frustration or anxiousness, the not-knowing, can be embraced as a tool to go deeper, to learn, as well as an opportunity to apply compassion.

*   *   *

I found that I would hold my work hostage to how I thought I should feel. I had to feel good or confident or in shape before I'd commit to doing the work. Then I discovered that when I get involved in the work, I am confident.

Bobby Lewis told us to turn our "ego worry into acting worry." When I plunge in, despite what's in my head, and allow the work to be confused and let myself be a "bad actor," I find that I've forgotten to be insecure. If I live out the moments without demanding to "know" or to see myself in a certain way, I engage my instincts and my acting comes from my gut—from me, from whom I am! The experience of the doing informs me instinctually beyond thought like what happens when a musician learns the notes.

My ego, though, will usually return to intrude; my habit is to slide into dualistic thinking: good writing/bad writing; good director/bad director; good actor/bad actor. In Zen, we call this ego the "small-self." It creates distance: I cling to my small self-conception of who I think I am, i.e., the only guy who's in the know and has the real goods. Ego. And then there is everyone else, the ones I'm competing against to win acceptance and approval. As if we're not in it all together wanting the same thing. It's unhappy and angry; it compares and gathers injustices. It creates suffering, which is called dukkha. It's all about my inabilities: all about me.

Lorraine Gessho Kumpf talks about how once in dokusan with Maezumi Roshi, after telling him how much she hated herself, he said to her, "You are so arrogant!" I thought that self-hatred was humility, when all that self-contempt, self-loathing, self-laceration—all that "self" stuff—is just that: only about me and it's driven by my compulsion to realize some idealized version of who I thought I needed to be to get what I want.

See the actor on the hamster wheel. Feel the Hungry Ghost's hunger. Without knowing it, I had turned acting into an existential referendum while creating a rift between me and the direct experience which was filled with suffering, dukkha.

*   *   *

"Nen" is a Japanese word that means a unit of thought or a steadily willed activity of mind. Zen sees consciousness as a continuous interplay between a sequence of three nen.

The first nen is the thing or activity itself. It is what it is. It is intuitive and direct: cold, door slam, cat.

The second nen immediately follows and is me saying in my head: "It's cold." Or "Loud door slam!" Or "kitty." It is the identification of the individual elements. It makes it an object of reflection. There is the direct experience, then the thinking about that experience. We label and become "aware." These secondary nen integrate and synthesize the preceding first nen into a continuous stream; this is how we become conscious of our thoughts.

And then the third nen is the inner discussion and interplay around the second nen! This is where reasoning, analysis, and introspection reside. "Who slammed the door? Is someone angry? I don't like slammed doors!" But there's a problem: this third nen is clouded by ego and promotes the false conclusion that all this thinking is the thing itself whereas it's only self-referential inner chat about itself. I create a smoke screen and buy into its obscurity. This is the delusion that interferes with the pure cognition that is the first nen, the thing itself, and it's where suffering resides; in the distance that my thinking creates.

In acting, the moment is that first nen. It just exists. It has integrity. It is what it is.

The second nen is when I observe and label the moment which leads to the third nen; all the talk, the assessing, the debate in my head between the opinions and judgements that come from all the watching that removes me from the direct experience which isn't about any of that. "It" just is. The moment doesn't need thought. The step in choreography or the note in music exists regardless of my opinion. It says in the ancient Buddhist text, *Affirming Faith in Mind*, "to pursue appearances is to miss the source...just let those fond opinions go." When I chase results and accept my internal commentary as the truth, I'm lost in an ego driven world of my own creation. The verses go on to say, "...cease to cherish opinions."

So this third nen, this "picking and choosing," is habitual and we accept it as true at the expense of what actually is, giving it space and granting it credibility. It is so ingrained that most of the time we aren't aware of its functioning. And if we become aware of this "picking and choosing we just might consider it essential. But it is not the truth. It is not the thing itself; the moment; the first nen.

In meditation, I don't have to tell my body to breathe. My body already knows how to do it and I just do it. Breath is the first nen. With acting, it is the moment, and I don't have to "do" it. I don't have to create it or comment on it or "make it work" or improve it. It is what it is. We give over to breathing in meditation; we give over to the moment in acting.

*   *   *

As we live the koan, it manifests as the expression of unity; I become the temple bell or the tree in the wind. I am past thought. When we live out the actions of the character, there is no gap, and we are the character. If my father is murdered by my uncle who then marries my mother and all I do is talk and talk and am incapable of doing anything about it, that's who I am.

If I truthfully realize, without thought, the action that the author has prescribed, that is who I am. I am the character. There is no separation. When we "just do," there is no division between subject and object. No you and me. No me and the character. We say:

Do it wholeheartedly.

Do it completely.

Be present!

No holding back or hesitation. No waiting for permission or to feel something first. Now. We do it with the fullness of our being. With the authority of doing it; no self, no self consciousness. Being one with.

Just.

Just listen.

Just say the line.

And as we go along and flounder and fail and struggle and agonize, we learn to accept that all of that is a part of it as well; the disappointment and messiness and fear.

We develop our humility like a muscle so we can perceive and accept what is happening in the moment; to truly leave ourselves alone and to keep going, to just keep going.

4

THE WORK: WASH YOUR BOWL

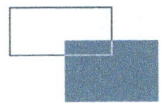

Do the next thing.
-Roshi Wendy Egyoku Nakao

My acting teacher and mentor, Freddie Kareman and I would speak every Sunday. I was in LA; he was in New York. He loved his Giants and Yankees and often a game would be on in the background and many were the times that he'd interrupt our talk to holler at Derek Jeter or Bill Parcells. We would talk New York, specifically West 72nd street where we'd been neighbors, and where he still lived, and we'd talk theater; he went to everything everywhere—small shows, Broadway shows, from Brooklyn to the lower eastside. Not only was he wholeheartedly devoted to theater, he had students, current and past, on stage all over the city. He'd tell me what excited him or disappointed him and eventually we'd always end up talking acting.

I'd ask questions and run teaching problems by him. He'd tell me to be myself, to teach from myself—that the trick was not to over-act, not to over-direct, and not to over-teach. And without fail, we'd arrive at "the work." He'd want to know was I really teaching "the work" and did I have any students who were "really doing the work?" And, most importantly, was anyone "getting the work?" Not that he would ever say it about himself, but Freddie had a mission; he was a caretaker of "the work." He was never not inspired about "the work."

Your parents take you to a play and it goes right through you and you fall in love and that's what you want to do, where you want to live. Without realizing it, you take a vow to do whatever you have to do so that you can spend your life up there on stage living in the magic you love. That love becomes the dedication and desire to get down to the acting in you. That is "the work."

The acting is in there. But what is it and how do I attend to it? How do I bring it out?

I cannot make anyone musical or give them rhythm. I can show them how to hold their hands or count but the musicality is in them. And no one can really teach anyone how to act. That's the first thing Bobby Lewis said to us! First class, we're sitting there all nervous and excited, in Bobby walked, looked at us and said, "No one can teach anyone how to act." Knock me over with a feather. After all the interviews and the waiting to get into the great man's class, he started with that!

You go to class hoping to learn the thing that's not teachable; to get down to the acting that's in you.

How does that happen?

What is that?

We teach ourselves by doing; learning is experiential.

I go to class and I fall on my face. Again and again. It's hard. I don't understand it. I overthink it. I push. I pout. I get cranky. But I pick myself up. I come back. I'm brave—remember Maezumi Roshi's "good guts?" That's how you do it.

The story goes that one day Balanchine came to watch class at the School of American Ballet, the academy for his company, and when the students were dancing the combination across the floor, skinny fifteen-year-old Gelsey Kirkland jumped so high she literally fell on her face. Her classmates tittered. The next day, Balanchine took her into the New York City Ballet where she went on to become one of the finest dancers in the world.

The illustrious piano pedagogue Rosina Lhévinne sent her students to Carnegie Hall to hear Arthur Rubinstein. When they came back, she asked them what they thought and when they said that he played a lot of wrong notes, she replied, "But <u>what</u> wrong notes!"

In an interview, Herbie Hancock remembered hitting a "wrong" chord while playing with Miles Davis: "Miles didn't hear it as a mistake, he heard it as something that happened, just an event, and so it was part of the reality of what was happening at that moment...He found something, since he didn't hear it as a mistake, he felt it was his responsibility to find something that fit. That taught me not only a big lesson about music but about life...The only way we can grow is to have a mind that accepts situations as they are and be able to turn them into medicine."

It takes strength and faith to become an actor. To do "the work" despite anything and everything. To fail over and over again and to get up over and over again; to learn by failing. In Zen, we say it takes great questioning, great determination, and great faith. In both acting and Zen, we keep coming back and we just keep going. We don't give up.

What does Nina say to Treplev at the end of Chekhov's *The Seagull*?

"...I've come to realize that in our work...the important thing is neither fame nor glamor...it's knowing how to endure. Know how to bear your cross and have faith. I have faith now and it's not so painful to me. And when I think about my profession, then I'm no longer afraid of life.[10]

There is a koan:

A monk said to Joshu, "Please teach me." Joshu asked, "Have you eaten your rice porridge?" "Yes, I have," replied the monk. "Then you had better wash your bowls," said Joshu.

Having eaten the porridge might mean, "Do you really see how things are? How we are all one together? Have you experienced that enlightenment?" And when the monk answers yes, he's saying that he has indeed had that insight. With acting, it could be, "Do you get it now? That it's about the work and not you?"

Washing the bowls can mean, "Having gained enlightenment, rid yourself of any pride about it—wash it away and keep going." Or simply, "Your bowl is dirty, it needs to be cleaned." For an actor: "Now that you understand that it's not about you, just learn your lines and show up."

Once, I was up against it and feeling desperate and I asked Roshi Egyoku straight out, "How do you do it? What's the answer?" And without missing a beat, she answered: "Just do the next thing." With acting it could be, "Be on time. Do your job as well as you can and go home." Freddie would tell us to just be "lunch pail actors."

---

[10] Anton Chekhov's Plays. P.49. Translated and edited by Eugene K. Bristow. Norton Critical Editions.

I always joke about what seemed to happen after every show regardless of whether we had gotten great notices or lousy reviews, if I had a flashy part or something small, my friends would come backstage and invariably say, "That was great, let's go eat." Didn't matter if I had just done Hamlet and opened the metaphorical vein, it was always, "let's go eat." Nice work, I'm hungry, let's do the next thing.

Wash your bowl.

Learn your lines and go to rehearsal.

Seek the stillness of not-knowing and the questioning, the great questioning of bearing witness. Welcome giving over to the action without thinking. Do the work with great determination.

When the job is not about me, I can be open to the depth of the experience and put myself at the disposal of the play. I will learn something beyond acting. I don't know what it will be but when I welcome the work with humility, it will be there and my acting will become about the human spirit—a spiritual lesson, if you will.

It's there waiting for me; a discovery about the world or myself or both. By forgetting myself, I am open to the hearts of the playwright and director and designers and the other actors and the audience. And I have faith in the questions and doubts. I have faith in the other actors, the director, the designers, the playwright and the play. I believe in the shared humanity and compassion of the work and of the theater. And this is something that I can carry out into the world.

Past ego and self-consciousness, past everything, all of it, there is the

moment.

Just the moment.

This very moment that all of us are dancing together. I give over to it and to you.

Simple human contact.

When we act, it's not only being of service to the play, it is an affirmation of our humanity and a gesture of love.

Simple human contact.

You and me here in this moment.

Simple human contact.

Call and response; pinch and ouch.

In Zazen, there is the breath. This breath. Then this one. Then this one. Then this one. And each time we take a breath, we breathe in the whole world. And each breath is a life. And each breath is exactly like a moment in acting.

Moment to moment to moment.

Breath to breath to breath.

Present, penetrable, alive, connected, human.

About the Author

Chris Fields is an artistic director, producer, director, teacher, actor, and Zen practitioner living in Los Angeles. He founded and is artistic director of the Echo Theater Company in Los Angeles where he has produced over a hundred premiere productions. As a director and producer, he has won Ovation, Los Angeles Drama Critics Circle, LA Weekly, and Stage Raw awards. He also founded and was artistic director of the Ojai Playwrights Conference. He began teaching in 1988 as an adjunct at the conservatory at the State University of New York Purchase and has had thousands of students since. As an actor he has appeared on Broadway, off-Broadway, regionally and in many films and tv shows working with many renowned directors and playwrights. Additionally, he was a member of the acting ensemble at The Eugene O'Neill National Playwrights Conference under the directorship of Lloyd Richards.

He began his Zen practice in 2008 at Great Dragon Mountain, Zen Center of Los Angeles. He received Jukai in 2010 and was given the name "Daian" – great ease. He is currently co-steward of the ZCLA instructors and tenzo circles.

www.chrisfieldsactingstudio.com
@chrisfields.actingstudio

"When I graduated from Yale Drama I didn't go near another acting class for 25 years. As an actor who has already developed my technique, I need to work my craft with someone who I trust to keep me honest, create a safe environment to work, and has a sense of humor. The acting teacher I go to is Chris Fields."

—*Christine Estabrook*
American Horror Story, Mad Men, Desperate Housewives

"Today, thanks to Chris I can call myself an actor. All it took was working professionally for twenty odd years, studying with some of the greats, and CHRIS, the only one who was able to put it all together for me and I guarantee he will do the same for you. No matter your background and experience or lack thereof, no matter your fears or excuses, no matter what your head tells you, Chris will nourish the actor in you so you can flourish and shine beyond your wildest dreams. (He'll teach you a thing or two along the way as well.) He is not only a friend, a mentor, but bar none the BEST acting teacher I've ever had the pleasure to work with."

—*Michael Massee*
Flash Forward, Revelations, Carnivale, 24

"In my humble opinion, what our art form (acting) lacks, is a degree of individual integrity that keeps the artist pursuing a mastery of their craft and to better themselves as human beings; there seems to be little interest in creating something beautiful, for it's own sake. Chris Fields has great integrity. He is an artist. He believes in the actor, the theater, and the human spirit. He is father, actor, director, teacher, and artistic director; all done with care and such compassion, you can actually see him bleed. Chris has directed me twice, and on both occasions he has guided me with tender and empowering hands, communicating his vision clearly and without hitting me over the head with lofty directions, we created something simple and true, both times. As a teacher, he'll not only give you the tools to apply in all your professional work, but he'll remind you of how special you are for what you do, and the great responsibility you have as an actor. He really is one of those people who want to create something beautiful for its own sake."

—*Enrico Colantoni*
Veronica Mars, Galaxy Quest, Person of Interest,
Just Shoot Me

"I studied with Chris Fields for years and I think he is one of the best acting teachers in LA. He works from a creative New York sensibility, but also keeps in mind the nuts and bolts of booking acting jobs in TV/film. The best of LA and New York combined into one teacher."

—*Danny Strong*
Buffy the Vampire Slayer, Justified, Mad Men,
Gilmore Girls, Recount (Emmy Nom and
WGA Winner),
Lee Daniel's The Butler (Oscar Nominated),
Chess on Broadway

"Chris Fields is a fantastic teacher and coach. His class provides a supportive environment to hone and develop skills and break habits. I have returned to Chris's class many times over the years between various characters and jobs to revitalize myself and give myself a clean acting slate. His class has definitely been an intrinsic part of my career and I'm very grateful."

—*Sprague Grayden*
Sons of Anarchy, Six Feet Under, 24

"Chris Fields is a wonderful artistic director, whose enthusiasm for new plays is absolutely contagious. He has built a force-field of joy and safety around Echo Theater, which is why playwrights like me trust him and call his office home."

—*Molly Smith Metzler*
Maid, Cry It Out, Shameless

"I have worked with Chris every opportunity available to me for the last eight years. I love the way he works with his actors, his insights into the characters and material and what the actor does with them and most of all the care and interest he shows for his students. He helped me tremendously and I am extremely grateful for all the time and effort he gave me and everyone else in class."

—*Mitch Pileggi*
Supernatural, Grey's Anatomy, Sons of Anarchy,
The X-Files

"When I have off between jobs I love taking scene study class with Chris Fields. He provides a safe environment to continue working on and experimenting with my craft while being guided by a teacher that understands that truth is the core of acting."

—*Peter Facinelli*
Twilight Saga, Nurse Jackie

"If you want to really work on your craft, go to Chris Fields. Chris' class is all about a practical approach to great material. He loves and respects actors and always has everyone's best interests at heart."

—*Emily Bergl*
Shameless, Southland, Desperate Housewives,
Men in Trees

"Artistic directors of theaters of all sizes would be wise to follow the [lead] of the Echo's Chris Fields, who [is] building audience communities eager for the challenge of path-breaking plays."

—Charles McNulty
Los Angeles Times

"I never took the time to thank you for everything you have done for me. It's really something I should have done before I left. I wouldn't be the actor, or the person for that matter, that I am if I hadn't been lucky enough to be introduced to your class. Before I worked with you, I always seemed to be a talented, natural actor who could pull some things off, but never really had a sense of why I was able to do what I do. I never really understood what it was to be truly emotionally connected to the reality of the situation. And all of a sudden everything opened up for me. You taught me how to act. Real acting. Not LA acting. I tried a couple other places before I found you and they were full of people who thought acting is crying or spending 3 hours at the gym everyday. But your class reminded me why I love doing what I do and that there are other people out there that feel the same way. And that's what will make the difference in everything I do. You have changed the lives of lots and lots of people and I hope that it's something that you don't take for granted. I watched a lot of people come through that classroom in the 5 years that I worked with you and everyone, myself included, improved by leaps and bounds. There are great directors and great teachers, but it's very rare to find them both in the same person. So thank you, Chris. Sincerely. Thank you for everything."

—Charlie Hirsch

www.ingramcontent.com/pod-product-compliance
Lightning Source LLC
Chambersburg PA
CBHW061702120626
46550CB00003B/1059